moldovan hotel

# moldovan hotel

### leah horlick

BRICK BOOKS

**Library and Archives Canada Cataloguing in Publication**
Title: Moldovan hotel / Leah Horlick.
Names: Horlick, Leah, author.
Description: Poems.
Identifiers: Canadiana (print) 20200389866 | Canadiana (ebook) 20200389890
ISBN 9781771315456 (softcover)
ISBN 9781771315463 (HTML)
ISBN 9781771315470 (PDF)
Classification: LCC PS8615.O745 M65 2021 | DDC C811/.6 — dc23

We acknowledge the Canada Council for the Arts, the Government of
Canada through the Canada Book Fund, and the Ontario Arts Council for
their support of our publishing program.

Canada Council    Conseil des Arts
for the Arts      du Canada

Canadian    Patrimoine
Heritage    canadien

ONTARIO ARTS COUNCIL
CONSEIL DES ARTS DE L'ONTARIO
an Ontario government agency
un organisme du gouvernement de l'Ontario

The author photo was taken by Erin Flegg.
The book is set in Carat.
Designed by Natalie Olsen, Kisscut Design.
Printed and bound by Coach House Printing.

**Brick Books**
487 King St. W.
Kingston, Ontario
K7L 2X7
www.brickbooks.ca

# Contents

11 For You Shall Be Called to Account

12 *In Rumenye Iz Dokh Gut*

13 A Shtetl, a Shtot

15 Annex

16 Two Villages

17 For Every Animal of the Forest Is Mine

18 Hodl

19 Curse for Bright Light

20 Ritual Instructions for Transnistria

21 Learning to Read Hebrew

25 You Are My Hiding Place

29 Return and Revive Us

30 *Aquila*

31 Census

32 Moldovan Hotel

38 Brief Conversation with Dybbuk, Strada Alexandru cel Bun

39 Every Name Means Across the River

41 Guilt

42 City of New Beginnings

43 Marginal Sea

44 Customs

49 Typhus

50 The Spinoza of Market Street

51 A Boy, a Girl, a Replacement

53 Couple Flying Over Village

59 Europe Eats Itself

60 Still Learning to Read Hebrew

61 *Barzel*

63 *Notes*    65 *Acknowledgements*    69 *Bibliography*

In Rumenye iz dokh gut
Fun keyn dayges veyst men nit
*In Rumania, life is good!*
*No one worries, no one should*

Aaron Lebedeff,
"Rumenye, Rumenye"

# For You Shall Be Called to Account

The ancestors of everyone I've let into my body
are gathered in a small room with one window,
no lights. Yes, the room is crowded. Yes, there
are no chairs. Yes, they are talking. *Why are we
here*, says the Nazi resister. *Where are the chairs*,
says the Viking (no horns). *Where is the light*, say
the people with their new French name hung
around their necks heavy like a long black cross.
*Here*, says the grand wizard, and a long white
light descends from a point on the ceiling.
The people of the oldest empire are here, too,
they have brought their own fire (hidden), they
too can speak French, they know in an instant not
to trust that light. They are opening the window.
*How do we get away from these people*, they
murmur. *True Aryans!* say the Nazis with their
new French name. No one is speaking
to the Catholics. There is a knock on the door —
there is a door. More Nazis. How did this happen?
Outside the open window there is a small huddle
of shawls and feet and candlesticks, a suitcase
and a cane. Someone has forgotten their things,
says the Nazi resister. The candlesticks turn into
my great-grandmother, their tarnish to coal smears,
the cane grows tall into my great-zayde, the shawl
his mother, suitcase an uncle with an aunt inside.
The feet are just empty shoes — my cousins have
already died. The small huddle of my family outside
the open window begins to sink to a great distance,
first one storey, then a long drop. Someone spits
through the open window. My great-zayde
shields his face. Great-Grandmother looks up.
*What are those people*, she says, *doing
in that room?*

## In Rumenye Iz Dokh Gut

*Everyone in these pictures looks like you!*
—childhood friend, upon reading her first book
about the Holocaust, circa 1996

You learn to use a word like a lock — how it
barely secures a mouth. A word

just far enough *east* that the elementary map
unrolls a little faded. Water spilled

across the collective atlas, childhood
reflex: *Romanian* — a word you throw

at people to make them go away.
A lock to shut many doors

at once. You tried turning it into a game —
*guess* — but everyone who was supposed

to win guessed wrong, again
and again, in the field, youth group,
security lineup. You cancelled

the tournament, but men
who miss home, drunk women — insistent
competitors, on sidewalks,

at the cash register, under neon — persisted
from across the street. The real
answer: shut your adult

mouth. It conceals one
song, two great-grandparents, one village,

one train, the valley of the shadow
of the Atlantic —

# A Shtetl, a Shtot

*The deader the language the more alive is the ghost.*
—Isaac Bashevis Singer

In another time I braid
and unbraid my hair

until the house falls down or
I get pregnant,

whichever happens
first. I worry

about teeth. In a circle
around the *shul* we stand —

the more important we are,
the farther away. Empire ticks

on slowly around us,
stealing our shoes and tailors and —

well —

everything. I spit out words
like seeds —

*hener, czar,*
*khasene.* Later, *tifus.*

I stand in the mirror, mutter —
I watch my face learn how to read

and then forget, then
never learn. It is hard

to imagine how dark it must have been
at night. A wool blanket, the pelt

of a beast. Great-Zayde
lights a lamp. Cuts a fake collar

from white cardboard, steps out onto
the broad back of the sky.

# Annex

*BASARABIA E ROMÂNIA*
—Graffiti slogan found across Romania. Reading "Bessarabia is Romania,"
it refers to territory annexed by Russia which now forms the Republic
of Moldova.

No matter your love for the trees, the colour blue,
    twilight comes to the forest. False border

between day and night and safety. Bessarabia calcifies
    around me, shatters and dissolves. Heralds electric light.

The only reason we know where we are is a bird call
    that screams from the future *That's not a real place anymore,*

over and over. The edge of Europe is a river
    that recedes from Ukraine saying *Get out now.* Somewhere,

a foundry begins to glow a faint fire. The air turns to smoke. Iron
    pulls itself back into the earth, dreading

a national purpose. I pull the forest around me and sprout needles,
    I pull the forest around me and grow knots, acacia bole,

soak up groundwater. Fade into a steppe
    and wait for death. Night is that bird call.

Night, your friend, the thief, is ruined. Night is
    a uniform, the earth who never turned you

away. Bessarabia collapses
    out of English — becomes spray paint

on an overpass, primary colours on cement,
    block letters crushed into a church.

Does the earth turn towards you or away? What do you call
    something you see everywhere, that tried to kill you,

but doesn't exist anymore?

# Two Villages

*after "Running Orders" by Lena Khalaf Tuffaha*

Red wrought iron,
blue roof.

White acacia,
yard full of chickens.

A knock on the door.
*This is David.*

First they confiscate our house,
give it to the neighbours,

if they don't kill us first.

Then they sell us to
the next country.

———

Red wrought iron,
blue roof.

Olive tree,
yard of almonds.

Roof-knock.
*David.*

First they confiscate your house,
give it to a bulldozer,
keep the tree.

If they don't kill you first then
they sell you
to another country,

still wearing the key to your house
around your neck.

# For Every Animal of the Forest Is Mine

*The round-up of the Jews [in Herta] was completed rapidly with*
*the aid of a local fiddler who was familiar with the Jewish homes.*
—"Policies and Implementation of Ethnic Cleansing in Bessarabia and
Bukovina," from *The International Commission on the Holocaust in*
*Romania: Final Report,* set up by Ion Iliescu and headed by Elie Wiesel

Later, when you said you were going to become a pastor, a forest
sprang up around us, blue-dark; the ceiling of the hostel
gave way to branches; the legs of the bedframe split down into roots.
You said you were really into being good to women, and my namesake
cousin with her lantern took a small step out of the trees. I moaned
and you thought I loved it, the forest of ruinous Europe invisible
to you, my cousin not yet damp with tuberculosis, how wonderful
this vision of my still-living name among instant old Romania,
village apparition, but her light did not touch the pool of our
blankets, I did not see her mouth moving through the shreds
of my clothes caught in the forest canopy. *You are safe, you are*
*cared for,* you said when I was on top of you and couldn't see
the crows shake their soft black heads. All of the good women
had left already — this wasn't fair to you either. Day coughed
into night and it was too late for me to leave the forest
and you had all of the good women and God in a cart
waiting for you on the road. And my future self could see
this from a glass city, not yet soaked with pneumonia, with
the ghost of my namesake cousin, we had just reached
through and pulled me out of those woods but when
I told you, I said the thing and you balked. *I can't*
*save you,* you said, and there I was again on a blanket
in the forest and you were leaving, everyone was leaving,
you felt unsuccessful. You left, our eyes wild, our yellow
teeth, all of us gleaming at you. The forest I pulled
around me, though neither the trees nor the road
were safe for women like me.

# Hodl

*after Isaac Bashevis Singer's "The Gentleman from Cracow"*

Did they call every kid in a rag heap
Lilith, or just the girls? Women bring misfortune, women light
the town on fire, women clean it up again. Women expected to be
the same, after the ashes, after we have held our own gold in our own
hands, worn silk, grown tired of being covered in chicken feathers
and flour. The girl in the rag heap — her absent father, bracelet of fangs,
money hidden in her skirt — knew what we didn't. When the devil
asked her *Have you sinned with Jews or Gentiles* she said *Both*
and when he asked her *Did you do it for money or for pleasure*
she said *Pleasure.* We burst into flames. There was no devil. Only
heat of sudden options. We lit the town on fire again
and with her braids she led us down the road
and we carried our gold
in our teeth.

# Curse for Bright Light

*For years, the CIA used a government building—codenamed "Bright Light"—
as a makeshift prison for its most valuable detainees…before they were
ultimately transferred to Guantanamo Bay… Unlike the CIA's facility in
Lithuania's countryside or the one hidden in a Polish military installation,
[Bright Light] in Romania was not in a remote location. It was hidden in
plain sight, a couple blocks off a major boulevard on a street lined with trees
and homes, along busy train tracks…The CIA shipped in Halal [sic] food to the
site from Frankfurt, Germany, the agency's European centre for operations.
Halal meat is prepared under religious rules similar to kosher food.*
—"Inside Romania's secret CIA prison," *The Independent*, December 8, 2011*

No one asked questions. It was
perfect—hide one government

within another. You kept it simple—water
and electricity. Threatened their mothers,

then pointed to the benevolent clock. Complained
your assignment wasn't *glamorous*, that they kept you

inside, too. No one ever thinks
they might be the serpent. In the next world,

may water and electricity turn away
from you. May you be brought to a place

everyone swears could not exist. *Impossible,
impossible.* May they decline

to comment. When you resist,
let them say *We checked your teeth,*

*we fed you,*

as they confiscate your memory of the ocean
while everyone around you nods,

bored of seeing your
orange jumpsuit
on the news.

# Ritual Instructions for Transnistria

*Avoid all travel to Transnistria, in northeast Moldova.*
—travel advisory from the Government of Canada, December, 2017

In your right hand, take the ten-hour tourist visa. Form a window with
your left, frame the last functioning hammer and sickle flag. Walk six
times around the last twenty thousand

tonnes of Soviet ammunition. A tanker spills cigarettes out of its side
like a whale and so we say *May the memory of this whale be a blessing.*
Wash your hands before you dunk your head

beneath the x-ray at the checkpoint, the x-ray that pretends not to notice
you. Rabbi, is there

a blessing for the border?

*A blessing for the border—*

May God bless and keep the borders, seen and unseen, far away from us.

# Learning to Read Hebrew

A shape is a door.

A door takes a different shape
if it comes at the end of the hall.

You can use your usual hand
to open the door, but if you reach

from the wrong direction,
the frame wavers, knobs
evaporate.

This door, well, the original lock
has been lost. We have to open it
another way. We make it work.

Many of these doors lead
to the same room. Many of them
only look the same, if you are not careful.

Some of them, despite being very old,
do not make even a single
sound.

*Regarding the Jewish matter*
*we do not work with written documents.*

Titus Popescu, captain under
Romanian dictator Ion Antonescu,
September 1941

# You Are My Hiding Place

The hole in the floor is old, old, old country.
It lives under the kitchen table, yawns wide

while the family eats, wider still when they starve.
Cold above, so below. When the horses march up to the house,

the hole — it has teeth — it chatters. Grandma says the hole
is where the women go when the Russians come.

Paramutation of hoofbeats. Epigenetic fur hats.
A long tablecloth, white-knit lace

brushing the floor.
If a black boot peeks under the lace.

If a sharp woolen shoulder leans down, suspects
a wooden floor, a hidden circle. Or

a dirt floor, a carefully dirt-covered
lid. If anyone sneezes. If a leather glove

lifts the lace, folds
the hole

into a tiny helix, leaves a switch
on a molecule, leaves

a boot print in a bomb shelter,
a gold button in the basement.

If a woman opens her hand decades later, reaches
for something, brushes away

webs of dust, stares
miles down

into the sudden circle
in her palm, says

*What the*
*hell is this*

*By the end of the 1930s, Romania's Legion of the Archangel Michael (often called the Iron Guard) became proportionately the third-largest fascist movement in Europe.*

Stanley G. Payne,
*A History of Fascism, 1914–1945*

*...Matthew Heimbach (a Catholic convert to Orthodox Christianity) was photographed wearing a т-shirt promoting Codreanu and the Iron Guard's Archangel Michael's Cross symbol in the aftermath of the August 2017 Charlottesville riots in Charlottesville, Virginia. [citation needed] The Archangel Michael's Cross was among the symbols emblazoned on the firearms used by Brenton Tarrant during the 2019 Christchurch mosque shootings.*

Wikipedia,
"Iron Guard," 2021

# Return and Revive Us

No one ever thinks they might be
the dragon.

Everyone wants to swing the
lance around, divine stomp.

A legion names itself
*protector,* prince among angels —

nested in green
shirts, scales on a beast.

Calls itself *iron.* Declares its task
*guarding.* Another legion

wraps itself in yards and yards of cloth,
whispers the name of that very

same deliverer. The archangel Michael

is confounded — intervenes
and appears, yanks humans out of the mouth

of the eternal lion as fast
as they throw themselves

in. *Archistrategos* is a web of light pulled
in the directions of his sparks. Starts

one fire. Beseeched to put it out again. Covers his ears,
leaves red handprints. Nobody thinks

they could ever be the serpent.
*Who is like God?*

# Aquila

The eagle doesn't mean
      to circle you. Its soft shadow

could span the back of the last aurochs,
      fossilizing in a watermelon field. The eagle didn't

ask for a cross in its beak, a crown, every point
      a sharp, narrow searchlight into the sunflowers.

To scythe through grass on blue dusk on grass, snap
      flat against a banner. It's not enough that we

have to rescue ourselves — who will deliver
      the eagles?

# Census

*The next day I hired a Yid to take us to Brichani... It turned out that there wasn't a single Russian in the town — they were all Jews, but there was nothing to be done; we rented an apartment from a Jew. The room was most unappealing, with a heavy and peculiar smell; my wife had never seen such a nasty chamber and it disgusted her. We lived there for over a week, and the boredom was unbearable.*
—excerpt from the autobiography of Nikolai Shipov, a Russian serf, published in 1881 in *Russkaia Starina*, a Russian journal of historical and memoir material

Brichan,
Bessarabia, 1897 —

ninety-six-point five percent
of the total population

Brichany,
USSR, 1940 —

Jewish population grows to about ten thousand
[dubious — discuss — citation needed]

Briceni,
Moldova, 2004 —

fifty-two Jews

# Moldovan Hotel

We count cattle, horses, the number of times
people at home said *I didn't even know that was a country —*

Soft sunset, reliable sunflowers.

I send photos home, subject:
*Guess if it's Saskatchewan or Moldova*

A field so yellow it could be canola. Tiny
silver dome of a church, sky over gravel.

Exposed bone
of communism. Old conversation,
unfinished. Gold teeth.

The first thing my parents ask me is
*Do you look like them*

The first thing someone says to us in English is

*You will have a good time in Moldova*

*It is very cheap for you and all the fruit is in season*

*Just do not talk to too many people you do not know*

———

It was dark, barely, blue
like a pigeon, the street — there was one paved street, trees
in Cyrillic shapes, just past the shadow of the border. And the carnival,

it was a whole block, rotating circles of light — if there was music, I don't
remember. We drove the length of Edineț in ten minutes, slowly, no
chirping

from the GPS since Romania, suddenly ancient, Ukraine decades away —
*This must be it.* A neon sign

says *Paradise.* A parking lot, a wedding. Creeping nausea across us like oil.
The gas station was a long time ago, twilight pulling

a little too close, miles since we cheered when the tiny black
pigs ran across the road. At last, reception — carpeted stairs, pulsing

techno, a clean shower. That sense of rattling across the grid, the gravel,
long after we had stopped. Every ten minutes I want to duck out to the lot

just to check on the car. We rub the dashboard and its white flank
like a beast, a beast on whom we entirely depend. Without it the little

village of you and me and our passports is no village.
Everyone listening in on our English is going to learn

*Where even* are *we? Where even* are *we!*

———

Anyone listening will hear me
practice *Edineț*, point to a map. Then,

quietly, *Yedinetz*. Like if I say anything

too loudly
in Yiddish

it will all come back.

———

In the Moldovan hotel, the Orthodox priest is our neighbour
now, as he probably was

my neighbour then. How heavy
is that wooden cross in this record

heat. Full night, now, day two of the wedding surrounds us. Two parents,
two violinists meet under the flowered arch near the parking lot. Some

old song wraps two fingers around my spine. Two parents
start to cry. The bride, a white nest

of tulle, smokes on a bench. Through the window, warm yellow light,
tall men in pale blue dress shirts are dancing, arms around
each other's shoulders. I am like a grenade

waiting to go off except instead of an explosion it's the *L'Chaim!* scene
from *Fiddler* with flashier lights and hookahs.

Except it's not a movie, it's a wedding.
And instead of our wedding,
it's theirs.

———

You and me and the little village of our passports, do we ever get drunk
and dance until late in the place where everyone was held

before all the Jews were marched to our deaths. Midnight, one o'clock —

I didn't know when we booked
the hotel. It was so close to the gravesite.

I hadn't even thought — proximity works
the same way it did seventy-five years ago.

Convenience.

When I wake up
early to someone banging on our door — the priest — who needs

a priest

this early — genetic relief —
it's not our door.

———

The wedding is over.
I didn't give any money to the woman waiting by the car

who was either related to me or killed my relatives.
There was no way to tell, I told
myself,
again.

———

Rattling back to the border, we parse
the bad feeling: the heat, language

barrier, too many movies
that look like this place,

or twelve thousand
Jewish spirits. There is no way to tell.

Poor Moldova — everyone keeps telling you to

fucking *smile*. Drinks your wine, turns around
and says it's not even that good. Everyone was so

kind to us — I mean, that man in a suit who arrived
at our door, sent by a friend in

Chișinău, who brought us champagne
and chocolate.

Maybe we laughed a little too loud
but everyone was so patient

with my emergency consonants, basic girl
phone voice: *Yeah it's going really well, so far*

*I'm pretty sure*
*they have no idea*

*I mean there's no way to tell*
*until I open my mouth*

———

The road sign, in Romanian,
is a word I've said in Yiddish

my whole life
without knowing —

the crucifix next to
the road sign.

(A whole country covered
in stone. A memorial — pile of unmarked

rock for Jews, circle out of rusted iron,
in the far corner, for the Roma.

Old men smoked and watched us touch
every part of it.)

We wade through the trees, setting stones
on the oldest graves — the same stones that

dropped from the graves like
apples. A tiny lizard
darts in and out of the grass.

How to explain to the cemetery keeper
why we're here:

I have one very old word that means *Hebrews*,
and the sound for a question. I hope someone

saw him offer us water under the tree.

Snake of a border shedding back and forth
across the ruined ground, except

a snake would be
natural.

———

It has been a long time
How long

doesn't really matter

I have come back
to drink your wine

I have come back to touch the trees
in the graveyard

I have come back
to use your shower

I have come back to stand
in this field

I have come back
to sing in the car

to drive the car

to drink your water
under the tree

I have come back
mostly to confuse you

I have come back
to drink your wine some more

This is just to say
*Nazdrovye, bitches*

I have come back
to close the gate behind me

# Brief Conversation with Dybbuk,
# Strada Alexandru cel Bun

Guiding the car over the broken street like a horse, two wheels
tilt at a time, shifting — the village becomes interlocking scales
of tin roof, a red

metallic fish, dead in the intersection. Seen from above it gasps
in the dust. The smell of it draws everything hungry for miles.
Old poltergeist, you've returned, you carry in your teeth that

bad joke about Vikings and villages. Squarely, see that another
set of helmets got here first but it's your thought that counts.
Safety was a wrought blue gate,

a yard, five thousand people rocking back and forth while the
border shuffled around them, rubbing letters in and out of
the mud on its forehead. Someone spoke and the mud went

everywhere. A gate became a fence, became a garden, a clock
tower, a genetic trap door that waited in my body saying
*Someday I'll be useful, just wait.* Thousands of miles away
you rattled

my whole nervous system so bitterly the generator behind
these houses choked, lit the street fluorescent white, without
explanation, midnight of winter. Bad star

on which I fixate, every new moon my gut rotates wildly like a
telescope, a mechanical eye, thrashes around to see if you still
hover above my life. Listen, fraction of *what happened* — look,

cortisol knot, root of why someone, somewhere is calling me
crazy — I was told to carry a stick to keep something like you
away. I know you followed me here. I was ready. I prepared

commands for you. *Sit. Stay.* Look at what lurked in the body of
my family all along. You had no idea what you were getting into,
did you.

# Every Name Means Across the River

*Govern there as if Romania had been ruling these territories for two million years. What will happen afterward, we'll see....*
—Dictator Ion Antonescu to Gheorghe Alexianu, head of the occupation regime of Transnistria, December 6, 1941

Dear cousins,
Your labour camp
is its own republic.

The mass grave wants
its independence.

The Soviets still
reach their long
arm across the river—

Abkhazia, Nagorno-Karabakh,
South Ossetia. Statues of dead
men who made

your dead
are everywhere.

When you hold your ear
above the river you can hear footsteps
pacing around and

around the Black Sea. Transnistria
has its own president

the same way Dachau
is a town—Dachau has always
been a town. It was easier

to visit. Children rode
their tricycles around and

around the camp. The nuns —
there were nuns there — they had taken a vow
of silence, a gold cross silent

on the roof, their long habits
sweeping the silent ground.

# Guilt

At first, like a head cold — then, three glasses of wine — no, five.
Hour twelve, a low-grade fever. Hour fourteen, your whole body is
on fire —

each joint snaps open, heat coiled inside your knees. A reaction to
the measles booster, days before the trip. Fades like a hangover,
then rears

its host of heads again. We choose not
to go to Chişinău — *We have no business*

*being here anymore.* Reroute to Iaşi. It's the heat,
driving stick, a last hiss,

writing to the chief rabbi

*I'm sorry we're not going to make it —*
*the GPS, the roads, Russian, the car*

which really means
*I'm sorry we are afraid*

# City of New Beginnings

*Has anyone ever seen a massacre of Jews in the streets of a German town?*
*We use the art of surgery, not of butchery!*
—Hans Frank, Nazi governor general of Poland, on the pogrom in Iaşi,
Romania, 1941


I hadn't wanted
to go to Iaşi. Do you ever wonder

if too much horror has happened
in one place. If it's better to just

treat it like the irradiated amusement
park, abandoned classrooms:

evacuate everyone within a thousand
square miles, let it break apart

like a Ferris wheel.

In twenty years, tourists would come
to feed the dogs, write their names

in the dust. Catch giant catfish
swimming in the dregs of the mikvah.

Teenagers would sneak across the wire
fence to drink, scuff around gravel, accidentally

find a meat hook in the dirt and run home
shivering. Some state agency would put up

a sign: *Too Many Terrible Things Happened Here.*
In fifty years, they get some funding, slowly

re-introduce us
into the habitat. *Who wants to live*

*around that many ghosts?* I ask, pulling
out my phone.

# Marginal Sea

Constanța is a benign myth after
fields on fields on iron on
loss. We counted every possible

symbol from Iași down —
this cow, this stork's nest, this
grandparent, this tasselled
horse. All of Romania flooded

with fog and light and sunflowers until
the ocean — really, a marginal sea. Absent-minded
oval, ocean's afterthought. A whole day in endless

procession to the water, the last inhale of lunar eclipse
draws a black swirl around our knees. We try to
take a photo by the single flame of a lighter, our faces

two red orbs. The sound is water on glass on
sand on legend, rattle and chime
of all the evil eyes for sale along the
boardwalk, still awake, blinking.

Under the drag-back is Ovid exiled among the fish,
Princess Anastasia, ghost of the monk
seals, two kinds of dolphins, one species
of porpoise. Zebra mussels, common carp.

We stand on the edge and wave
to all the countries so close we can feel
them turn in for the night —

*Good night Armenia!*
*Good night Iran!*
*Good night Azerbaijan!*

I have been carrying a lot of waves I promised
I would deliver. Heavy eyelid of Europe, propped
open by the road sign pointing to Istanbul. One by one
the Argonauts roll over in their sleep.

## Customs

In the dream I can draw the whole
country — the route from Otopeni

past the cement plant, stands
of poplars, the sky

fuchsia, coarse
with bare branches, gravel

stretching ahead like a summer — I've driven
into the drawing. My family is safe at the lake

of my childhood — warm in the evergreens. They smile
as I drive across the grid to Moldova like it

makes perfect sense. In the cement plant
parking lot I stop to make sure I have

my papers. With an inhale the sky is brushed
over with a blue sponge. Oh it's going to be

*dark* soon. A miscalculation. I imagine beams
of headlights in a field,

sleeping in the car. Inside the cement plant it's a hotel
and everyone can understand me because I am wandering around

asking *Vamă?* the one word that came with me into
the dream. You can't just drive between two countries

like you're driving over a line. Only one more
day in subconscious Romania — *What a shame,*

*I've come all this way. Oh well. I saw*
*the graveyard last time.* I should go back, I think,

I'm going to get in the car and drive back
to the lake of my family. This is unsafe. I don't

have to do it. I imagine driving up
to the cabin, the little circle of spruce, my parents —

*It was getting dark! I didn't*
*leave enough time.*

*Regarding the Jewish problem, it can be established that a man like [Ion] Antonescu acts in this field in a more extremist manner than we have done so far.*

Adolf Hitler to Joseph Goebbels,
August 1941

# Typhus

God forbid — it's a terrible
way to go. Vector of rats

and possums, lice and fleas. *Jail fever. Hazy
delirium.* I have lived in the city long

enough to learn a few things DDT
was good for. I learn that the Nazis got so angry

at the Romanians because they just left the dead
Jews in piles, didn't bury or burn them, and we

spread typhus into the groundwater, then to the Nazis.
Because I am gay I don't believe in disease as metaphor

or punishment. It is hard to know what to believe
anymore. It is hard to be the people on

either side of the conspiracy — the moon landing
is not the same as the opioid crisis is not the same as

a docile forest monster, not the same as the CIA. I had hoped
not to grow up to be an old woman writing haltingly to some

church to say *We regret to inform you that your archbishop
was a Nazi,* but here we are.  It is hard to learn anything

at first about typhus because I have to scroll through
the weeds of fascists saying *no no, it was all just*

*the disease, no one was ever made to dig their own grave
in the trees.* Through the screen I can hear hundreds

of miniature online Reagans laughing
at each briefing about AIDS *It's not murder*

*if everyone gets sick.*

# The Spinoza of Market Street

*after Isaac Bashevis Singer*

I know better now. I have eaten
a great deal of dust, felt my feet on the
floor of rooms on rooms on
quiet, pale green rooms. I have been

listening to my body for a long time now
and there is a lot of bad music in there
I never have to listen to again. Two psychics

have told me to wait for you, provided specifics,
hair colour. I have rented a room in the tower and plotted
stars. My skin is soft with the grease from candles. I carry my copy
of *Trust After Trauma* with me everywhere and it is kind of

a joke now, it helps. I keep watch
for you in the courtyard. Fights break out,
carriages rattle past like giant locusts, then the war.

The glass in my windows is faceted
and dark. This time I will wait until we have known
each other for a long time, and when I come to you at night

I will pull silk dress after satin dress out of
my chest and say *This is my trousseau* and

you will be impressed with me, I have such
a careful inventory of my things.

# A Boy, a Girl, a Replacement

*There is a saying that Jewish families should have three children —
one to replace each parent, and one to replace the children lost in
the Holocaust.*

The third child will not open her eyes at first, like a kitten. On
the seventh day, she lifts each lid slowly. Every eye the Black Sea.
Already there are circles. She says *This is the world now*, walks
out the front door. The third child does not crawl.

The third child is indestructible — bike accidents, kitchen counters,
impossible trees. She bites the ashen thermometer, gnaws smoky
lead. A little cold, a little blue, just a scratch.

Eats everything in her path, remains rail-thin, refuses to wear
stripes. Does not grow hair, and then a cascade. Curls like vines
fall out, then burst into flames.

The third child watches her older siblings sleep — little cherubs,
binary replicas of her parents, each a whole covenant. Mimics
their docile breath, their flutter of lash from her perch.

Handful, her voice cracks, shatters. Nightly a whole host cries out
from her throat. Sometimes a small chorus, like frogs, pubescent
cantors. When the Gentiles say *hello* on the street — the roar of a
train, a piercing whistle.

The third child's bat mitzvah goes on for hours. A procession of
young women walks in and out of her mouth, *finally*, now's their
chance, a corona of shimmering mothers surrounds her, *geyshoyn*.

*your golden hair Margarete*
*your ashen hair Shulamith*

But the third child's mother? Adherent in the front row, fenced
by other parents and their fresh duets of children. She ignores

the hiss, the crooked finger. Her third child, her jewel — a legion of ghosts in her body, little stigmata.

The third child's mother, calm as doves. God has already told her, told everyone about her daughter — an uncountable body of stars.

# Couple Flying Over Village

*Do you want to go away from here with me? We'll be together days*
*and nights at a time. Your father won't be there, nor your mother...*
*Nobody'll scold you...or beat you... We'll be all by ourselves...*
*For days at a time... We'll be so happy. What do you say, Rifkele?*
—Manke to Rifkele, Act III, *God of Vengeance* by Sholem Asch,
translated from Yiddish

There must have been so many
daughters, all these women braiding

everything soft while their husbands write
from Kiev or Lvov or —

never call, never write. Scores of
Sheyne-Sheyndels-in-waiting. It must

have been very dark and very
quiet at night. And with all the men

in a field, the back room, or
studying ten hours a day. Someone sneaks

down into the brothel, the cellar, goes out
into the rain in her nightgown. She's *taking a bath.*

She's *washing her hair.*
There's no way

everyone had a dowry. And the rabbis mostly agreed — you could even
still marry a rabbi. *Whither thou goest*

and all that. *Your people will be my people,*
I swear, holding up a little lantern

behind the shtetls,
drifting over all the tiny

houses — a red roof, a blue window, trying to
see what we must have missed.

It can't be all rainwater
and Shabbat scenes,

I know. It's called
*God of Vengeance.*

I don't care. Blessed art thou, historical
flicker of self that mandates neither

chickens nor husband,
twelve children. Flicker of lamplight,

real money, more than one
dress. A voice that asks

*do you like this*
*you'll be the bride*

———

Through the trap door
I insist on, Madam/Mother pays everyone
off. Sends her daughter with

the candlesticks, what's left
of a scroll. A figure waits

for her by the lamppost. I pretend
they make it to Kiev, Bucharest,

Odessa — they look

at the sea. Sell
everything for the train ticket,
get on the boat. *She's my*

*cousin.* Whither thou goest. Boston,
New York.

———

We are surrounded by
the other ending—

parents' house inescapable. Winter
apocalyptic. Scant miles
insurmountable. Manke dissolves

into a cascade of letters. A border
rears its sudden head, the tail
of the beast knocks over

a village. Rivkele becomes a series
of concentric red circles in the newspaper.
If you are not careful

they will have you thinking
we were incandescently

alive until the clock
reached 1940. Like the shtetl

was some little museum, tiny
Jews clucking along

beneath a glass case, invincible.

———

I pretend that before the arrest, this first-ever
kiss onstage is a bottle cracked

over the hull of the city. Shabbat is for
kissing. I like to think of two

very old women in a tenement, busy learning to play
mah-jong, easing their knees up the stairs.

I dream of a headline that shouts
*Indecency!* hung on the wall like a trophy

next to a scroll.

In 2008, two ethnic Hungarian members of the Romanian
Parliament demanded the banning of Romanian ultra-
nationalist group Noua Dreaptă (The New Right) on the
grounds that it continues Iron Guard's spirit. The members
of Noua Dreaptă revere Corneliu Zelea Codreanu, leader
of the Iron Guard, and refer to him as "Căpitanul"
("The Captain"), which is what Codreanu's supporters
called him during his lifetime.

adapted from the Wikipedia page
for "Noua Dreaptă," 2017

During a 2018 interview with alt-right Mormon blogger
Ayla Stewart, the Canadian white nationalist Faith Goldy
recommended Codreanu's book For My Legionaries —
which explicitly called for the extermination of the Jews —
calling it "very, very, very, very spot on, given a lot of
what the movement is talking about right now"; she later
said she no longer endorsed the book.

Wikipedia,
"Iron Guard," 2021

# Europe Eats Itself

Europe inhales sharp and folds in
on itself. Its shoulder is a triple cross

stamped with iron, one elbow
is a flag

held the wrong way
on purpose. Europe has no teeth

left, gnaws its leg, eats itself
dead. A regime explodes,

becomes a statue, becomes a ruin,
becomes a joke. Then it kills

you. A border grows a fence,
a fence grows a hole, a hole for endless

cars and cigarettes and taxes
and weapons and people, becomes

a weapon itself, was always
a weapon. Becomes the Mediterranean.

How is anyone going to swim
in that ever again? I can't stop thinking about

the kid I remember from
history class who could take apart

an AK-47 in thirty seconds.
We all thought
*dope*

## Still Learning to Read Hebrew

The tail of a letter knocks on a window. Behind
     the window, there is a watch.     ׅ

The watch has been stuck and it will start
     to tick again. Time

was stopped — someone shoved
     a book in front of me as a child and said

*Can't you read this,* letters swimming like
     tadpoles. No one told me even long stretches

of ancestors, right to left, couldn't. I made sounds I didn't
     understand, watched how the light fell, swayed.

The letter ק swoops in, left to right. Whispers
     *Don't worry, you can learn this later.*

# Barzel

*The Hebrew word for iron,* barzel, *is an acronym for four of the mothers of the Children of Israel.*

When I come back, I can control it.

Instead of my whole body collapsing
       into a cart—held together by bones, drawn

by some creature
       halfway like a lizard—

I open and close myself,
       a safety pin. Silver-plated back

of an earring. I carefully monitor
       my own blood.

When I come back and other people cross me,

they smell iron and are swept
       like dust back onto

a dirt road. They appear in a ring
       of white acacia. In the dark they are

surrounded by thorns. One step, instant scream
       of a rusted gate.

It only lasts a few seconds.

No one is really sure if they felt it. See them jump,
       like there's been a loud noise, except there wasn't.

When I come back, every time

someone threatens me I open my hands—
       two extra sets of eyes, blinking. Another two

watch from the creases of my elbows. Like mirrors,
       they reflect all the fear back into each wooden body.

# Notes

I created *Moldovan Hotel* during a period of escalating neofascist
violence worldwide. Each poem was written and re-written
while holding the following dreams in my body: a world without
antisemitism, a world where Muslims travel without restriction,
of freedom and right of return for Palestinians, of the day when
the Iranian people are released from sanctions, a world without
internment camps, and the dream of sanctuary and safe passage
for migrants worldwide. During my research it was also impossible
to ignore how much work remains to be done even to simply
recognize historic and ongoing attempts at the destruction of the
Roma and Sinti peoples, and the global impact of antiziganism.

The title "For Every Animal of the Forest Is Mine" is from Psalm
50:10. The line "as they confiscate your memory of the ocean /
while everyone around you nods" in "Curse for Bright Light"
refers to "Ode to the Sea," an exhibition of work by detainees
at Guantánamo Bay curated by Erin Thompson, Paige Laino,
and Charles Shields. The "blessing for the border" sequence in
"Ritual Instructions for Transnistria" references the "Is there a
blessing for the Tsar?" scene in *Fiddler on the Roof.* "You Are
My Hiding Place" is from Psalm 32:7. "Return and Revive Us"
is from the Rashi commentary on Psalm 85. The archbishop
referred to in "Typhus" is Valerian Trifa. The lines "your golden
hair Margarete / your ashen hair Shulamith" in "A Boy, a Girl, a
Replacement" are from Paul Celan's *"Todesfuge."* "Couple Flying
Over Village" refers to a Marc Chagall painting entitled "Over the
Town." "Sheyne-Sheyndels-in-waiting" is a reference to Sheyne
Sheyndel, a character featured in the stories of Sholem Aleichem.

May the names of all oppressors throughout this text be blotted out.

# Acknowledgements

These poems were written on the unceded territories of the
xʷməθkʷəy̓əm (Musqueam), Skwxwú7mesh (Squamish) and Selı́lwitulh
(Tsleil-Waututh) peoples. Indigenous land defenders and water
protectors on each coast and across many territories preserved
the world in which I wrote these poems, and our future, countless
times during the creation of this book.

Brick Books and River Halen Guri provided astonishing support for
this manuscript from acquisition to publication. I'm unspeakably
grateful for the deep consideration and abundance of attention
they showed to each difficult facet of this work.

An early version of this project appeared as "Mikvah," a long
poem anthologized in *You Care Too Much*, beautifully edited
and encouraged by Erin Klassen (With/out Pretend, 2016). Early
versions of "Couple Flying Over Village" and "You Are My Hiding
Place" were shortlisted for the 2018 *Arc* Poem of the Year prize,
for which "You Are My Hiding Place" was named the winner.
Thanks to Chris Johnson and the jury for this tremendous honour.
An early version of "A Boy, a Girl, a Replacement" was longlisted
for *PRISM international*'s 2017 Pacific Spirit Poetry Prize, with
thanks to editor Jessica Johns and the jury. "For You Shall Be
Called to Account" and "For Every Animal of the Forest Is Mine"
first appeared in *Nimrod International Journal*'s fall 2016 issue,
"Mirrors and Prisms."

Alex Leslie provided invaluable first draft edits and cabbage
rolls for this project from its inception, and connected me with
the community at Or Shalom, which was also recommended
to me by Sigal Samuel. Courses by Rabbi Hannah Dresner and
Rahel Halabe filled many painful gaps in my Jewish knowledge.

Elee Kraljii Gardiner and Juliane Okot Bitek gave me tremendous advice on travelling for difficult research. James Funk and Dr. Silke Falkner supported me in developing a lifelong love of the German language and its literature, and thus prevented me from becoming hopelessly lost in Moldova. Behshid Zojajpour Foadi and her entire family offered me profound care throughout the writing process, sharing their love of poetry, thoughtful discussion, and much-needed laughter. While writing *Moldovan Hotel* I relied on advocacy work and commentary on world events by the Jews of Color Caucus with Jewish Voice for Peace, and the Twitter feeds of Rabbi Danya Ruttenberg (@TheRaDR) and Rebecca Pierce (@aptly_engineerd) for my continued education, as well as emotional and spiritual resources.

I am grateful to the members of the International Commission on the Holocaust in Romania for their 2005 Final Report, and for making the text available online in English. Citations from this invaluable document are used throughout.

This book would not have been possible without the three-phase cemetery restoration project conducted in Briceni by volunteers with the JewishGen Bessarabia Special Interest Group and Online Worldwide Burial Registry. The dignity and care they devoted to the graves of our people — and their careful online and photographic documentation — is truly a gift.

It's a Jewish tradition to dedicate a period of study to a departed ancestor or teacher. Everything I learned through the process of writing *Moldovan Hotel* is dedicated to the memory of the following formidable minds in my Jewish education: Rabbi Roger Pavey, Dr. Martha Blum, Dr. Elizabeth Brewster, and especially my departed grandparents Dr. Louis Horlick, Ruth Horlick, and Douglas Power, whose memories are truly a blessing.

My grandmother Sylvia Power (née Schuster) has preserved countless memories and stories that are the foundation of this text, now and forever. This book is for her, and our family. My parents, Anna and Allan, and my brother Nicholas and his fiancée Allison, were so brave to walk into this difficult project together with me. I hope I answered some of our questions; I'll keep at it.

My trip to Romania and Moldova was funded by the Canada Council for the Arts, who made it possible for me to become the first woman in my family to return since the Holocaust. Amy Huziak did not even blink when I asked her to join me; she was my co-pilot and steady, bright star the entire way. *A sheynem dank.*

# Bibliography

I read widely for the creation of this text. Views expressed by the authors of these sources should not be assumed to be necessarily congruent with mine.

Ancel, Jean. *The History of the Holocaust in Romania.* University of Nebraska Press, 2012.

Asch, Sholem. *The God of Vengeance: Drama in Three Acts.* The Stratford Company, 1918. https://archive.org/details/godofvengeance drxooasch

Bauchina, Alisa. Simon Erhardt. Martin Franke. *A Day in Transnistria.* 15 October 2015. https://www.youtube.com/watch?v=HoZxvr2NjDA

Butnaru, Ion C. *The Silent Holocaust: Romania and Its Jews.* Greenwood Press, 1992.

"Corneliu Zelea Codreanu." *Wikipedia: The Free Encyclopedia.* https:// en.wikipedia.org/wiki/Corneliu_Zelea_Codreanu

Dorman, Joseph. *Sholem Aleichem: Laughing in the Darkness.* Riverside Films, 2011.

Friling, Tuvia. Radu Ioanid. Mihail Ionescu (eds.). *International Commission on the Holocaust in Romania: Final Report.* Polirom, 2005.

Geidner, Chris. "13 Times The Reagan White House Press Briefing Erupted With Laughter Over AIDS." Chris Geidner. *Buzzfeed.* 2 December 2013. https://www.buzzfeednews.com/article/chris geidner/times-the-reagan-white-house-press-briefing-erupted-with

Gilbert, Martin. *Letters to Auntie Fori: The 5,000-Year History of the Jewish People and Their Faith.* Schocken, 2002.

Goldman, Adam. Matt Apuzzo. "Inside Romania's Secret CIA Prison." *The Independent.* 8 December 2011. https://www.independent.co.uk/ news/world/europe/inside-romania-s-secret-cia-prison-6273973.html

"Iron Guard." *Wikipedia: The Free Encyclopedia.* https://en.wikipedia. org/wiki/Iron_Guard

Kogan, Yefim. "The Jewish Cemetery of Briceni." 2019. https://www. jewishgen.org/Bessarabia/files/cemetery/briceni/BriceniCemetery.pdf

MacKay, John. *Four Russian Serf Narratives.* University of Wisconsin Press, 2009.

Mlotek, Avram. "A Look Inside Jewish Romania." *Forward.* 16 December 2016. https://forward.com/scribe/356942/a-look-inside-jewish-romania/

"Ode to the Sea." *Art From Guantánamo Bay.* 3 April 2020. https://www.artfromguantanamo.com/.

Oișteanu, Andrei. *Inventing the Jew: Antisemitic Stereotypes in Romanian and Other Central-East European Cultures.* University of Nebraska Press, 2009.

"Only in the Chimney: Anti-Semitic Carol Causes Uproar in Romania." *Spiegel Online.* 12 December 2013. https://www.spiegel.de/international/europe/romania-anti-semitic-christmas-song-causes-uproar-a-938703.html

Oster, Marcy. "Romanian dictionary to change slur's definition." *Jewish Telegraphic Agency.* 10 August 2011. https://www.jta.org/2011/08/10/global/romanian-dictionary-to-change-slurs-definition

Payne, Stanley G. "A Unique Death Cult." *Slate.* 21 February 2017. https://slate.com/news-and-politics/2017/02/romanias-unusually-morbid-fascist-movement-blended-nationalistic-violence-with-fanatical-christian-martyrdom.html

"Recommended Reading." *Sholem Aleichem.* https://sholemaleichem.org/recommended-reading/

"Redefining racism: Romanian dictionary corrects anti-Semitic and anti-Roma words." *National Post.* 26 April 2012. https://nationalpost.com/news/redefining-racism-romanian-dictionary-corrects-anti-semetic-and-anti-roma-words

"Romania: Monitoring and Combating Antisemitism." *Somondo.* https://www.somondo.org/organizations/1279/mca-romania-monitoring-and-combating-antisemitism

*Romania: Poverty Made In Europe.* https://www.arte.tv/en/videos/076893-000-A/romania-poverty-made-in-europe/

"Roumania, Roumania: How It Sounds." *How It Sounds.* 29 March 2017. https://isaacwritesaboutmusic.com/category/how-it-sounds/

Singer, Isaac Bashevis. *The Collected Stories.* Farrar Straus Giroux, 1982.

Tuffaha, Lena Khalaf. *Water & Salt.* Red Hen Press, 2017.

"Talking around a subject." *Friar Yid.* 11 August 2011. http://friaryid.blogspot.ca/2011/08/talking-around-subject.html

*Yiddish Song — Belz, Mayn Shtetele Belz.* 5 April 2009. https://www.youtube.com/watch?v=88pCBld3TVk

Leah Horlick grew up as a settler on Treaty Six Cree territory and the homelands of the Métis in Saskatchewan. Her first collection of poetry, *Riot Lung* (Thistledown Press, 2012), was shortlisted for both a ReLit Award and a Saskatchewan Book Award. In 2016 she won the Dayne Ogilvie Prize, Canada's only award for LGBT emerging writers. That same year, her second collection, *For Your Own Good* (Caitlin Press, 2015), was named a Stonewall Honor Title by the American Library Association. In 2018, her piece "You Are My Hiding Place" was named Poem of the Year by *ARC Poetry Magazine* and shortlisted for inclusion in the 44th Pushcart Prize by the Pushcart Board of Editors. She lives on Treaty Seven Territory & Region 3 of the Métis Nation in Calgary.